D1632098

contents

tapas

THE ESSENTIAL KITCHEN

introduction

To the average Spaniard, the local tapas bar provides the three things held dearest good food, good wine and the opportunity to offer an opinion in convivial conversation. Much of Spain s social and business conversation is held in caf s and bars, and no one would dream of a drink without *algo para picar* something to nibble at; in other words, tapas.

The word *tapa* literally means lid, and the origin of the tapas custom most probably lies in the placing of a small plate or lid over a glass of wine when served. It is also said that a centuries-old decree insisted all bars and roadhouses serve food as an accompaniment to wine, in an attempt to ensure at least a modicum of sobriety among the nation s coach drivers.

Whatever its origins may have been, the daily gathering before lunch or dinner for the ritual partaking of tapas, as both an appetizer and an adjunct to conversation, is now an integral part of the Spanish way of life. Tapas have evolved into an almost separate style of cuisine.

Some areas of Spain, such as the waterfront barrios of Barcelona, seem to contain little else but tapas bars, each offering its own specialty. Some serve half a dozen dishes, others as many as seventy or eighty. Whether the bars of Barcelona or the *tascas* of Madrid or any other Spanish city or town, these establishments are individualized by the origins of their proprietors. It is almost impossible to go anywhere in Spain without encountering both Basque and Galician tapas bars boasting a rich offering of seafood and shellfish dishes. Who could forget a first encounter with *Pulpo a la Gallega* (Octopus Galician Style) or any one of the dozens of clam and mussel dishes, not to mention the myriad ways of preparing squid and the smell of shrimp (prawns) grilling in garlic and olive oil on the *plancha* (griddle). These seafood dishes from the Bay of Biscay states are the ones most easily adaptable abroad. But not to be overlooked are the Moorish-influenced dishes of the south, like *Pinchos Morunos* (Moorish-Style Kabobs), or the rich heritage of the peninsula s interior, such as a real Spanish omelette, along with recipes for meat, game, poultry, beans, chickpeas and hundreds of different sausages and pies. The Mediterranean coast and the Balearic Islands also have an incredible variety of seafood and meat dishes.

Bars also advertize themselves according to the conversational predilections of their patrons, whether it be discussing jai alai, bullfights, soccer, arts or politics. Running a tapas bar seems to be a noble form of retirement for past sporting heroes.

Tapas are a tradition long peculiar to Spain, but the last two decades have seen their growing popularity in the United States, particularly New York and California, and internationally, where the proliferation of tapas bars is a testament to the public s willingness to embrace the nation known for a more sensible social style of drinking. Tapas, while remaining quintessentially Spanish, lend themselves easily to adaptation.

Many recipes in this book are authentically Spanish. You ll also find exciting variations. When serving tapas, try presenting them in Spanish crockery. You might have Spanish classical guitar music playing in the background to help create the slightly eccentric conviviality of an authentic Spanish tapas bar.

Buen provecho!

STEP-BY-STEP

techniques

Empanada pastry

The filled pastries known as empanadas come in many varieties. Not only are they common in Spain but they can also be found throughout Central and South America. The secret of getting empanadas right is having the filling mixture at the right consistency and the pastry at the right temperature.

A good filling should be reasonably thick, with no oil or liquids exuding from it (which would make it difficult to join the pastry edges together). The filling should be cold so that it doesn t soften the dough. It s best to keep the pastry circles in the refrigerator, filling only four or five at a time.

Although homemade pastry produces an admirably better result, already-prepared empanada pastry is available in Spanish and South American delicatessens. You can also use a commercial puff or short pastry; the type that comes in rolled sheets is already the approximate thickness required for empanadas. After you have cut out the circles, let them rest in the refrigerator for at least 30 minutes and take out just a few at a time as described below.

9 cups (2¼ lb/1 kg) all-purpose (plain) flour
approximately 2 cups (16 fl oz/500 ml) cold water
generous pinch of salt
1 lb (500 g) butter, at room temperature

Makes enough for 60 empanadas

1. Pile flour on a pastry board and make a well in center. Gradually mix in enough water to make a smooth, workable dough, adding salt at some point during this process. Knead dough for at least 7—8 minutes, continually turning and folding it back onto itself. Wrap dough in plastic wrap and let rest in refrigerator for at least 30 minutes.

2. On a floured board, roll out dough into a large, thin sheet. Spread butter (which should be room-temperature soft, but not melting) evenly over dough. Fold edges into center at least 4 times. Wrap and return dough to refrigerator for 30 minutes.

3. Again roll out dough on floured board and fold over at least 8 times. Return to refrigerator for another 30 minutes, then roll dough to 1/16 inch (2 mm) thick and cut into 4-inch (10-cm) circles. Press scraps together and roll into additional circles. Lightly flour circles and return to refrigerator for 30 minutes. Bring them out 4 or 5 at a time to fill.

4. Place 1—2 teaspoons filling in center of each circle. Fold in half and pinch edge between your thumb and forefinger, turning edge inward to ensure that filling remains enclosed.

Marinated olives

Aceitunas aliñadas

Green olives

8 oz (250 g) canned or bulk green olives, pits intact
12 large cloves garlic, crushed
1 tablespoon chopped fennel bulb
olive oil as needed

Drain off any liquid from olives and lightly crush olives. Put in a sealable glass jar with the garlic and fennel. Pour in olive oil to cover. Cover and store in refrigerator, turning occasionally. Serve at room temperature.

Black olives

8 oz (250 g) black olives, pits intact
2–12 cloves garlic, crushed
1–2 dried red chili peppers
red wine vinegar as needed
dash of lemon juice

Drain off liquid from olives and lightly crush olives. Put in a sealable glass jar with garlic to taste and chilies. Pour in red wine vinegar to cover and add lemon juice. Cover and store at room temperature for at least 3 weeks.

Piquant olives

8 oz (250 g) large green olives
8 green chili peppers
white wine vinegar as needed
dash of lemon juice

Remove pits from olives and place in a sealable jar with chili peppers. Pour in white wine vinegar to cover and add lemon juice. Store at room temperature for at least 3 weeks. These olives are a favorite in Spanish tapas bars and are great appetizers with predinner drinks.

Tip

The secret of marinating your own olives is to leave them marinating as long as possible—a minimum of three weeks and a maximum of six months.

Roasted Peppers

Pimientos Asados

Roasted peppers (capsicums) are used on their own, as an integral part of many other dishes and as a garnish. If served whole as tapas, it is best to use small peppers. When the peppers are used as an ingredient or garnish, they are invariably cut into thin strips or are finely diced. They also make an excellent addition to chicken or seafood salads. For a stand-alone dish, you will need 6 red bell peppers. Serves 6

1. Brush peppers with olive oil and bake in a 350—400¡F (180—200¡C/ Gas 4—6) oven for about 30 minutes. Alternatively, roast on a charcoal grill or a stove-top grill pan for a shorter time.

2. The peppers are cooked as soon as they collapse and portions of the skin are blackened.

3. Place peppers into a plastic bag or wrap in aluminum foil. Seal and stand for 10 minutes. Remove, peel and seed peppers.

4. Toss with a dressing of olive oil, a little lemon juice and salt and pepper. If you wish, add a bit of anchovy, chopped onion and parsley.

Stuffed artichokes

Alcachofas rellenas

8 artichokes
olive oil as needed
½ cup (3 oz / 100 g) minced onion
8 oz (250 g) ground (minced) lean pork
3 oz (90 g) ground (minced) ham
½ cup (2 oz / 60 g) breadcrumbs
2 tablespoons chopped fresh parsley
salt and freshly ground pepper
Zesty tomato sauce (see page 56)

Trim top $^{3}{}_{4}$—$1^{1}{}_{4}$ inch (2—3 cm) from artichokes. Bring a pot of salted water to a boil, add artichokes and cook until tender (do not overcook). In a frying pan over medium heat, warm about 1 tablespoon olive oil. Add onion, pork and ham and fry until pork is barely cooked. Remove from heat and drain off any excess fat. Add breadcrumbs, parsley, salt and pepper, and mix well.

Pull leaves of each artichoke outward to expose prickly choke. Remove choke, being sure to leave heart intact. Fill each artichoke with stuffing.

Preheat oven to 350¡F (180¡C / Gas 4). Cut stem from each artichoke so artichoke will stand upright. Arrange artichokes in a baking pan. Sprinkle with a little olive oil and bake for 20 minutes. Serve hot with zesty tomato sauce.

Serves 8

Stuffed artichokes II

Alcachofas rellenas II

Trim top $^{3}{}_{4}$ inch (2 cm) from artichokes. Bring a pot of salted water to a boil. Add vinegar and artichokes and cook until artichokes are tender (do not overcook). Refresh in cold water.

In a frying pan over medium heat, warm half of olive oil. Add onion, ginger and garlic and fry for 2—3 minutes. Stir in flour and cook for 1 minute, stirring constantly. Add tomato and bell pepper purees and simmer for 10 minutes.

Meanwhile, melt butter in another frying pan over medium heat. Add shrimp and cook only until they have changed color. Refresh in cold water.

Season tomato mixture with salt and pepper. Add cognac and cook for 5 minutes, then let cool. Add eggs, breadcrumbs, diced pepper and shrimp.

Pull leaves of each artichoke outward to expose prickly choke. Remove choke, being sure to leave heart intact. Fill each artichoke with shrimp stuffing.

Preheat oven to 475¡F (240¡C / Gas 9). Cut stem from each artichoke so it will stand upright. Arrange artichokes in a baking pan. Sprinkle with remaining olive oil and bake for 10—15 minutes. If desired, sprinkle with Parmesan cheese about 5 minutes before removing artichokes from oven. Serve hot with zesty tomato sauce.

Serves 8

8 medium artichokes
2 tablespoons white wine vinegar
3 tablespoons olive oil
1/2 cup (2 oz / 60 g) finely diced onion
1 1/2 teaspoons minced fresh ginger
1 1/2 teaspoons minced garlic
1 tablespoon flour
1/2 cup (4 fl oz / 125 ml) tomato puree
1 large red bell pepper (capsicum), roasted, peeled and seeded (see page 9), then pureed
1 tablespoon butter
1 lb (500 g) shrimp (prawns), peeled and chopped
salt and freshly ground pepper
1 tablespoon cognac
2 eggs, lightly beaten
1/2 cup (2 oz / 60 g) breadcrumbs
1 large red bell pepper (capsicum), seeded and finely diced
grated Parmesan cheese (optional)
Zesty tomato sauce (see page 56)

Fried eggplant with Parmesan cheese

Berenjenas con queso

- 2 medium eggplants (aubergines)
- 2 eggs
- 4 cloves garlic, minced
- 1/4 cup (2 fl oz / 60 ml) water
- 1 cup (8 fl oz / 250 ml) olive oil
- flour as needed
- 7 oz (220 g) Parmesan cheese, finely grated

Cut eggplants into batons 2 inches by $^{1}{}_{2}$ inch (5 cm by 12 mm). In a bowl, mix eggs, garlic and water. In a frying pan over medium-high heat, warm olive oil. Dredge eggplant slices in flour, dip in egg mixture and then dip in cheese, making sure both sides are coated. Fry until golden brown, about 2 minutes on each side. Drain on paper towels. Serve immediately.

Serves 8

Hint

You may want to keep one batch of fried eggplant warm in the oven while you work on the next, but if left too long, the eggplant will turn soggy.

Stuffed eggplant

Berenjenas rellenas

To make herbed tomato sauce: In a frying pan over medium heat, warm olive oil. Add onions, garlic and ginger and fry for 3 minutes. Add tomatoes and cook for 10 minutes. Puree in a food processor, then add basil and cilantro. Measure 1 cup (8 fl oz / 250 ml) sauce; set aside remainder.

Preheat oven to 475¡F (240¡C / Gas 9). Cut eggplants in half lengthwise and deeply score flesh in a crisscross pattern, being careful not to cut skin. Use 2 tablespoons of oil to coat flesh, then place slices on a baking sheet and bake until almost cooked through, 8—10 minutes. Scoop out flesh, leaving a shell about $^{3}{}_{8}$ inch (1 cm) thick. Puree flesh and set aside.

In a frying pan over medium heat, warm 1 tablespoon of olive oil. Add onion and garlic and fry for 3 minutes. Add celery and bell pepper and cook for 3 minutes. Add reserved tomato sauce and eggplant puree and cook for 5 minutes. Remove from heat and stir in flour and breadcrumbs. Let cool for 10 minutes, then fold in egg whites. Season with salt and pepper.

Stuff eggplant shells with tomato mixture and place in an oiled baking dish. Cover half of each stuffed eggplant with Parmesan cheese. Bake until browned, 10—15 minutes. Spoon remaining sauce over other half of each eggplant and garnish with basil sprigs.

Serves 8

FOR HERBED TOMATO SAUCE
1 tablespoon olive oil
2 large onions, finely chopped
4 cloves garlic, finely chopped
1½ teaspoons peeled and finely chopped fresh ginger
1 lb (500 g) fresh or canned tomatoes
chopped basil, to taste
chopped cilantro (coriander), to taste

4 small or medium eggplants (aubergines)
¼ cup (2 fl oz / 60 ml) olive oil, or as needed
1 large onion, finely chopped
6 cloves garlic, finely chopped
1 celery stalk, finely chopped
1 red bell pepper (capsicum), seeded and finely chopped
1½ tablespoons self-rising flour
1 cup (4 oz / 125 g) fresh breadcrumbs
2 egg whites, beaten
salt and freshly ground pepper
2 tablespoons freshly grated Parmesan cheese
basil sprigs, for garnish

Mushrooms with bacon

Champiñones con tocino

1 tablespoon olive oil
4 oz (125 g) diced tocino or bacon
2 cloves garlic, finely chopped
1 lb (500 g) button mushrooms
1/2 cup (4 fl oz / 125 ml) dry white wine
salt
2 teaspoons freshly ground pepper
1 tablespoon chopped parsley

In a frying pan over high heat, warm olive oil. Add tocino and fry for 3 minutes. Add garlic and mushrooms and stir well. Add wine, salt, pepper and parsley and cook over high heat until most of wine has evaporated and mushrooms are cooked, 3—4 minutes. Serve hot.

Serves 6

Mushrooms in garlic and parsley

Champiñones al ajillo

1/4 cup (2 fl oz / 60 ml) olive oil
6 cloves garlic, finely chopped
1 lb (500 g) mushrooms
2 tablespoons chopped parsley
1 tablespoon flour
1 cup (8 fl oz / 250 ml) water
salt and freshly ground pepper
juice of 1/2 lemon

In a frying pan over medium heat, warm oil. Add garlic and fry for 1—2 minutes, making sure garlic doesn t burn. Add mushrooms and parsley and cook until mushrooms begin to exude liquid.

Add flour and stir constantly until liquid becomes a paste, then stir in water, salt, pepper and lemon juice. Simmer for 10 minutes, adding a little more water if sauce is too thick. Serve hot.

Serves 6

Stuffed mushrooms

Champiñones rellenos

Heat olive oil in a frying pan large enough to hold mushrooms. Add garlic, then mushrooms, tops down, and saut gently until browned but not cooked through, about 2 minutes. Remove mushrooms.

Add onion and tocino to pan and saut for 2—3 minutes. Pour off any excess liquid. Add parsley, remove from heat and let cool. Add eggs and breadcrumbs and mix well. Stuff mushroom caps with tocino mixture and top each with Parmesan cheese. Broil (grill) or bake in an oven preheated to 450¡F (230¡C / Gas 9) until cheese is browned and mushrooms are cooked through. Serve at once.

Serves 8

¼ cup (2 fl oz / 60 ml) olive oil
1½ teaspoons finely chopped garlic
32 button mushrooms, about 2 inches (5 cm) in diameter, stems removed
1 tablespoon finely chopped onion
¼ cup (1 oz / 30 g) minced tocino or bacon
1 tablespoon finely chopped parsley
2 eggs, lightly beaten
2 tablespoons fresh breadcrumbs
2 tablespoons freshly grated Parmesan cheese

Potato salad

Ensaladilla

6 potatoes, boiled, peeled and diced
½ cup (2 oz / 60 g) diced cooked carrot
½ cup (2 oz / 60 g) cooked green peas
1 cup (8 fl oz / 250 ml) Garlic mayonnaise (see page 56)
salt and freshly ground pepper
1 red and 1 green bell pepper (capsicum), roasted, peeled and seeded (see page 9), then cut into strips
parsley sprigs, for garnish

In a bowl, mix potatoes, carrot, peas, mayonnaise and salt and pepper to taste. Mound on a platter, top with pepper strips and garnish with parsley. The flavor will improve if the salad is left standing for an hour at room temperature.

Serves 8

Hint

This mayonnaise-and-potato salad, found in every tapas bar in Spain, is invariably one of the first dishes to be presented each day. It begins as a highly decorated mound of salad on a large platter and diminishes as the day progresses.

Potatoes in spicy sauce

Patatas bravas

Preheat oven to 475¡F (240¡C / Gas 9). Heat 4 tablespoons of olive oil in a frying pan over high heat until smoking. Add potato and brown thoroughly. Transfer potatoes and oil to a baking dish and bake until potatoes are crisp, about 15 minutes.

Meanwhile, heat the remaining 1 tablespoon oil in a frying pan over medium heat and saut onion and garlic for 3 minutes. Add remaining ingredients and simmer sauce for 10—12 minutes. Drain potatoes and place in a serving bowl or individual dishes. Pour sauce over potatoes and toss there should be just enough sauce to coat. Serve at once.

Serves 8

5 tablespoons olive oil
8 large potatoes, peeled and cut into 1½-inch (4-cm) cubes
1 large onion, finely chopped
3 cloves garlic, finely chopped
2 tablespoons finely chopped parsley
3 fresh chili peppers, seeded and chopped, or 1 tablespoon chili sauce (see page 56)
2 cups (16 fl oz / 500 ml) canned plum (Roma) tomatoes, pureed
½ cup (4 fl oz / 125 ml) dry white wine
salt to taste
chorizo or chopped bacon to taste (optional)

Spinach pastries

Empanadas de espinacas

- 1 tablespoon olive oil
- 2 cloves garlic, finely chopped
- 2 tablespoons finely diced chorizo or ham (optional)
- 1 large bunch spinach, stemmed, washed and chopped
- 1 red bell pepper (capsicum), roasted, peeled and seeded (see page 9), then cut into strips
- salt and freshly ground pepper
- empanada pastry (see page 7)
- 1 egg beaten with 2 teaspoons water

Heat oil in a frying pan over medium heat. Add garlic and chorizo and fry for 1 minute. Add spinach and toss until wilted. Add bell pepper strips and remove from heat. Let cool. Squeeze out any liquid from spinach mixture. Season with salt and pepper. Put 2 teaspoons spinach mixture in center of each pastry circle, remembering to take circles from refrigerator only 4 or 5 at a time. Fold circles over filling and crimp edges. Refrigerate for at least 15 minutes.

Preheat oven to 475¡F (240¡C / Gas 9). Arrange empanadas at least $^{3}{}_{4}$ inch (2 cm) apart on a greased baking sheet. Brush with egg wash. Bake until golden brown, 5—6 minutes. Serve immediately.

Serves 8—10

Fish pastries

Empanadas de pescado

Heat oil in a frying pan over medium heat. Add onion and garlic and fry until transparent. Add tomato, chili and salt and pepper to taste and cook until somewhat thickened. Add parsley and diluted tomato paste and cook for 3—4 minutes. Remove from heat and let cool. Mix in fish, egg and bell pepper.

Preheat oven to 475¡F (240¡C / Gas 9). Put 2 teaspoons fish mixture in center of each pastry circle, remembering to take only 4 or 5 circles from refrigerator at a time. Fold circle over filling and crimp edges. Refrigerate for at least 15 minutes.

Arrange empanadas at least 3 4 inch (2 cm) apart on a greased baking sheet. Brush with egg wash. Bake until golden brown, 5—6 minutes. Serve immediately.

Serves 8—10

2 tablespoons olive oil
1/2 cup (2 oz / 60 g) finely chopped onion
2 cloves garlic, finely chopped
1 large tomato, chopped
1 red chili pepper, seeded and chopped
salt and freshly ground pepper
1 tablespoon chopped parsley
1 tablespoon tomato paste diluted with a little water
8 oz (250 g) cooked and boned firm-fleshed fish such as tuna or cod
1 hard-boiled egg, chopped
1 red bell pepper (capsicum), roasted, peeled and seeded (see page 9), then diced
empanada pastry (see page 7)
1 egg beaten with 2 teaspoons water

Chorizo and olive empanadas

Empanadas de chorizo y aceitunas

- 2 oz (60 g) chorizo, finely chopped
- 1 oz (30 g) pimiento-stuffed green olives, finely chopped
- 1 tablespoon finely chopped red bell pepper (capsicum)
- 24 empanada pastry circles (see page 7)
- 1 egg beaten with 2 teaspoons water

In a bowl, mix chorizo, olives and bell pepper. Put 1—2 teaspoons chorizo mixture in center of each pastry circle, remembering to take only 4 or 5 circles from refrigerator at a time. Fold circle over filling and crimp edges. Refrigerate at least 15 minutes.

Preheat oven to 475¡F (240¡C / Gas 9). Arrange empanadas at least $^{3}{}_{4}$ inch (2 cm) apart on a lightly greased baking sheet. Brush with egg wash. Bake until golden brown and pastry is cooked through, about 5 minutes. Serve immediately.

Serves 6—8

Spicy shrimp and scallop empanadas

Empanadas de mariscos picantes

In a frying pan over medium heat, melt 1 tablespoon of butter. Add chopped shrimp and scallops and gently saut until shrimp change color (they should not be cooked through). Place in a colander, refresh under cold running water and set aside.

In a frying pan, melt remaining 1 tablespoon butter and saut onion, garlic and ginger for about 3 minutes. Add curry powder and flour and cook, stirring constantly, to make a roux, about 3 minutes. Add coconut cream, cilantro, salt (if using) and chili sauce and cook for 3—4 minutes, stirring to make sure mixture is smooth. Add shrimp and scallops and immediately remove from heat. Let mixture cool.

Preheat oven to 475¡F (240¡C / Gas 9). Put 2 teaspoons seafood mixture in center of each pastry circle, remembering to take only 4 or 5 circles from refrigerator at a time. Fold circle over filling and crimp edges. Refrigerate for at least 15 minutes. Arrange empanadas at least $^{3}{}_{4}$ inch (2 cm) apart on a greased baking sheet. Brush with egg wash. Bake until golden brown, 5—6 minutes. Serve immediately.

Serves 8—10

- 2 tablespoons butter
- 8 oz (250 g) jumbo shrimp (king prawns), peeled and chopped
- 7 oz (220 g) scallops, chopped
- 1 onion, finely chopped
- 2 cloves garlic, finely chopped
- 1½ teaspoons peeled and finely chopped fresh ginger
- 1 tablespoon hot Madras curry powder
- 1 tablespoon flour
- ½ cup (4 fl oz / 125 ml) unsweetened thin coconut cream or coconut milk
- 1 tablespoon chopped fresh cilantro (coriander)
- salt (optional)
- 1½ teaspoons chili sauce (see page 56), or to taste
- empanada pastry (see page 7)
- 1 egg beaten with 2 teaspoons water

Andalusian baked eggs

Huevos a la flamenca

- 2 tablespoons olive oil
- 1 onion, finely chopped
- 2 cloves garlic, finely chopped
- 1 lb (500 g) canned whole peeled plum (Roma) tomatoes, coarsely chopped
- 1 cup (6 oz / 180 g) diced serrano ham or proscuitto
- 2 chorizo sausages, cut in rounds 3/8 inch (1 cm) thick
- 12 eggs
- 24 pencil-thin asparagus spears, blanched
- 1 red bell pepper (capsicum), roasted, peeled and seeded (see page 9), then cut into strips
- 1 tablespoon finely chopped parsley
- freshly ground pepper

Heat oil in a frying pan over medium heat. Add onion and garlic and fry for 3 minutes. Add tomatoes and cook for 10 minutes. In a separate pan over medium heat, cook ham and chorizo for 3 minutes.

Preheat oven to 400¡F (200¡C / Gas 6). Divide tomato mixture among 6 individual ramekins. Break 2 eggs into each ramekin and then arrange ham, chorizo, asparagus spears and bell pepper strips around them. Sprinkle with parsley and season with pepper. Bake until egg whites are cooked but yolks are still runny, about 10 minutes. Serve at once.

Serves 6

Hints

As the name suggests, this dish has its origins in Andalusia, the southern province of Spain, which is home to a large proportion of the country's gypsy population. You can vary this dish by adding a tablespoon of chili sauce (see page 56) to the tomato mixture. You can also give it a sprinkling of Parmesan cheese, but don't overdo it.

Spicy hard-boiled eggs

Huevos duros picantes

In a large frying pan, warm oil over medium heat. Fry garlic, ginger and onion until onion is transparent. Add ground spices and chili and cook for another 2 minutes, stirring constantly. Remove from heat and allow to cool.

Blend onion-spice mixture in a food processor with coconut cream. Return mixture to pan and bring to a boil. Add eggs, reduce heat to low and simmer for 30 minutes, stirring occasionally. Serve garnished with cilantro sprigs.

Serves 8

2 tablespoons olive oil
2 cloves garlic, finely chopped
2 teaspoons peeled and finely chopped fresh ginger
1 onion, finely sliced
1 teaspoon ground cumin
1 teaspoon ground coriander
1 teaspoon ground turmeric
1 tablespoon seeded and chopped red chili pepper
1½ cups (12 fl oz / 375 ml) unsweetened thin coconut cream or coconut milk
8 hard-boiled eggs
cilantro (coriander) sprigs for garnish

Salmon-stuffed eggs

Huevos duros rellenos

- 6 hard-boiled eggs
- 1 can (3–5 oz / 90–150 g) red salmon, drained
- 6 green olives, pitted and finely chopped
- 2 tablespoons mayonnaise
- 1 teaspoon paprika
- 1½ teaspoons chopped parsley
- 2 teaspoons lemon juice
- salt and freshly ground pepper
- 1 slice smoked salmon, cut into thin strips
- 1 green bell pepper (capsicum), seeded and cut into thin strips

Halve eggs lengthwise. Remove yolks and reserve 4 for another use. Place remaining 2 yolks in a bowl and add remaining ingredients except smoked salmon and bell pepper. Blend well.

Transfer yolk mixture to a pastry (icing) bag and fill egg whites with mixture. Arrange smoked salmon and bell pepper strips on top.

Serves 6

Eggs with tuna mayonnaise

Huevos con mayonesa de atún

- 8 hard-boiled eggs, halved lengthwise
- 1 can (3 oz / 90 g) tuna, drained
- 1½ cups (12 fl oz / 375 ml) Garlic mayonnaise (see page 56)
- 1 tablespoon lemon juice
- 16 anchovy fillets
- 1 red bell pepper (capsicum), roasted, peeled and seeded (see page 9), then cut into strips
- watercress sprigs, for garnish

Place 2 egg halves, yolk side down, on each serving plate. Press tuna through a fine-mesh sieve into a bowl and add mayonnaise, a little at a time, whisking until combined. Add lemon juice. Thickly coat eggs with tuna mixture. Top with anchovy fillets and bell pepper strips and garnish with watercress sprigs.

Serves 8

Spanish omelette

Tortilla española

In a heavy nonstick frying pan about 10 inches (25 cm) wide and with sloping sides about 2 inches (5 cm) deep, heat 2 tablespoons of olive oil over high heat. (Adjust quantities as necessary if using another pan size.) The secret of this recipe is a very hot pan. When oil begins to smoke, add potatoes, a few pieces at a time, until pan bottom is covered one layer deep. Top potatoes with a layer of onions. Repeat until all potatoes and onions are used. Cook, turning frequently, until potatoes are tender, then remove from heat and transfer potatoes and onions to a large bowl. Clean pan thoroughly.

In a large bowl, whisk eggs with a little salt. Mix into cooked potatoes and onions. Add 1 tablespoon of oil to pan and reheat until oil is smoking. Pour egg mixture into pan and stir away from pan bottom until half of egg is cooked, pressing onions and potatoes into mixture. Shake pan and run a spatula around side and bottom to make sure omelette is not sticking. When omelette is cooked three-quarters of the way through and bottom is browning (do not allow to burn), place a large plate over pan and invert omelette onto it.

Quickly clean pan and add a little more olive oil. Slide omelette back into pan, uncooked side down, and cook until firm throughout. Turn out onto a serving dish and let stand for 5—10 minutes before cutting into wedges. In Spain, it is served lukewarm or at room temperature.

Serves 12—16

3 tablespoons olive oil,
  plus extra as needed
5 potatoes,
  peeled and thinly sliced
2 large onions, thinly sliced
15 eggs
salt

Hints

The Spanish omelette is, without a doubt, the country's most commonly served dish. A true Spanish omelette contains only three main ingredients: potatoes, onions and eggs, plus salt and the oil in which it is cooked.

Mushroom omelette

Tortilla de champiñones

3 tablespoons olive oil
1 onion, finely chopped
1 lb (500 g) mushrooms, sliced
12 eggs

Heat 2 tablespoons of olive oil in a frying pan about 8 inches (20 cm) wide and with sloping sides about 2 inches (5 cm) deep over medium heat. Saut onion and mushrooms for 4—5 minutes. Meanwhile, in a bowl, beat eggs with salt and pepper. Transfer onions and mushrooms to a strainer lined with a paper towel and drain thoroughly, then add to eggs.

Wipe pan, return to medium heat, add remaining 1 tablespoon oil and heat until smoking. Add egg mixture and stir away from pan bottom 5 or 6 times. Cook until omelette is set two-thirds of the way through, shaking pan to make sure eggs don t stick. Place a large plate over pan and invert omelette onto it. Slide omelette back into pan, uncooked side down, and cook until set throughout. Divide into 12 equal portions and serve.

Serves 12

Zucchini omelette

Tortilla de calabacines

In a covered steamer set over boiling water, steam zucchini until tender but not soggy, about 3 minutes. Alternatively, cook in $^{3}{}_{4}$ inch (2 cm) boiling water for 3 minutes. Drain.

In a large bowl, beat eggs with salt and pepper to taste. Heat 1 tablespoon of oil in a frying pan about 8 inches (20 cm) wide and with sloping sides about 2 inches (5 cm) deep over medium heat. Add onion and garlic and saut for 2—3 minutes. Drain and add to eggs along with zucchini.

In the same pan, heat remaining 1 tablespoon oil until smoking. Pour in egg mixture and stir away from pan bottom 5 or 6 times. Cook until omelette is set two-thirds of the way through, place a large plate over pan and invert omelette onto it. Slide omelette back into pan, uncooked side down, and cook until set throughout. Divide into 12 equal portions and serve.

Serves 12

10–13 oz (300–400 g) zucchini (courgettes), cut into slices about $^3/_8$ inch (1 cm) thick
12 eggs
salt and freshly ground pepper
2 tablespoons olive oil
$^1/_2$ cup (2 oz / 60 g) finely chopped onion
1 clove garlic, finely chopped

Spicy shrimp omelette

Tortilla de gambas picantes

- 3 tablespoons olive oil, plus extra as needed
- 2 large potatoes, peeled and thinly sliced
- 1 large onion, thinly sliced
- 15 eggs
- 1 teaspoon salt
- 4 red chili peppers, seeded and chopped, or 1 tablespoon chili sauce (see page 56)
- 2 cups (12 oz / 375 g) peeled, deveined and chopped jumbo shrimp (king prawns)

Heat 2 tablespoons of olive oil in a pan about 6—8 inches (15—20 cm) wide and with sloping sides about 2 inches (5 cm) deep over medium heat. When oil begins to smoke, spread half of potatoes evenly in pan, top with onion and then add remaining potatoes. Turn mixture frequently until potatoes are cooked; take care not to burn them. Remove from heat.

Beat eggs with salt in a bowl large enough to hold all ingredients. Stir in chilies, shrimp and potato mixture.

Wipe pan clean, add remaining 1 tablespoon oil and heat until smoking. Add egg mixture and stir away from pan bottom 5 or 6 times. When omelette is half cooked, reduce heat, shake pan and run a spatula around side to prevent omelette from sticking. When omelette is almost cooked, place a large place over pan and invert onto it.

Return pan to high heat, making sure nothing is sticking to it, and add more oil if needed. Slide omelette back into pan, uncooked side down. Reduce heat and cook until omelette is set throughout. Invert onto a plate and let stand for a few minutes before cutting into wedges. Serve warm or, as is more typical in Spain, at room temperature.

Serves 8

Stuffed red peppers

Pimientos rellenos

Preheat oven to 400¡F (200¡C / Gas 6). Brush bell peppers with a little olive oil, place on a baking sheet and roast for 15 minutes. Cut around stem of each pepper, pull it out and reserve. Remove seeds.

Heat 2 tablespoons olive oil in a frying pan over medium heat and saut onion and garlic until transparent. Add tomatoes and chilies and cook until reduced to a smooth sauce. Add mussels, clams, parsley, and salt and pepper to taste. Remove from heat and add rice.

Preheat oven to 375¡F (190¡C / Gas 5). Stuff peppers with rice mixture. Do not overfill as rice needs room to expand. Replace stems. Arrange peppers in a baking dish and brush with a little olive oil. Bake until heated through, 10—15 minutes. Serve hot.

Serves 6—8

6–8 small red bell peppers (capsicums)
2 tablespoons olive oil, plus extra for brushing
1/2 cup (2 oz / 60 g) chopped onion
2 cloves garlic, finely chopped
3–5 oz (90–150 g) canned tomatoes, finely chopped
2 red chili peppers, seeded and chopped
12 mussels, cooked and diced
1 can (8 oz / 250 g) whole clams, drained
1 tablespoon chopped parsley
salt and freshly ground pepper
1/2 cup (2 oz / 60 g) cooked white rice

The ingredients used in many traditional Spanish dishes differ from household to household, bar to bar, restaurant to restaurant or region to region. It is possible to order a dish in ten different places and receive ten different versions, even though all have the same name on the menu. Pimientos Asados (Roasted Peppers) is one such dish. This is one of the most popular versions in Spain.

Potato and ham croquettes

Croquetas de patata y jamón

- 2 tablespoons butter
- 2/3 cup (3 oz / 90 g) ground (minced) ham
- 1 1/2 teaspoons flour
- 1/2 cup (4 fl oz / 125 ml) milk, plus extra as needed
- 1 tablespoon chopped parsley
- salt and freshly ground pepper
- 3 large potatoes, boiled and mashed
- dash of lemon juice
- flour, for dredging
- 2 eggs, beaten with a little water
- breadcrumbs, for coating
- oil, for frying

Melt butter in a frying pan over medium heat, making sure it doesn t burn. Add ham and heat gently for 2 minutes. Stir in flour and then add 1/2 cup (4 fl oz / 125 ml) milk, parsley and salt (omit if ham is salty) and pepper to taste. Cook for 1 minute. Stir in mashed potatoes and then lemon juice.

If potato mixture is too dry, add a little more milk, but take care not to add too much liquid. Let mixture cool, then refrigerate for at least 1 1/2 hours or up to 2 days.

Form croquettes in a cylindrical shape 3 inches (7.5 cm) long and 1 inch (2.5 cm) in diameter. Roll in flour, dip into beaten eggs and then coat with breadcrumbs. For best results, refrigerate croquettes for at least 30 minutes.

In a frying pan, heat enough oil to cover croquettes. Oil is ready when a bread cube dropped in hot oil sizzles on contact. Fry croquettes, turning once, until golden brown. Drain on paper towels and serve immediately.

Serves 6

No Spanish tapas bar is complete without at least one variation of the ubiquitous croquetas. Whether they are made from ham, chicken, shrimp (prawns), fish, vegetables, meat or even rice, they invariably have one of two foundations: mashed potatoes or a flour-and-milk dough that is crumbed and fried. Either way, they are delicious. This first recipe is made with potatoes. When frying croquettes, make sure oil is hot enough; if it isn't, the croquettes tend to fall apart.

Seafood croquettes

Croquetas de pescado

Melt butter in a frying pan over low heat. Stir in flour and cook, stirring constantly, for 2—3 minutes; make sure the roux doesn t burn. Little by little, whisk in milk and wine. Add paprika and salt and pepper to taste and whisk until mixture is completely smooth.

Stir in fish, shrimp and parsley and cook for 5 minutes. Remove from heat and stir in mussels. Let mixture cool, then refrigerate for at least 3—4 hours or, preferably, overnight.

Shape seafood mixture into croquettes about 3 inches (7.5 cm) long and 1 inch (2.5 cm) in diameter. Roll in flour, dip into beaten eggs and then coat with breadcrumbs. For best results, refrigerate for at least 30 minutes.

In a frying pan, heat enough oil to cover croquettes. Oil is ready when a bread cube dropped in hot oil sizzles on contact. Fry croquettes, turning once, until golden brown. Drain on paper towels and serve immediately.

Serves 12—15

7 tablespoons butter
1 cup (4 oz / 125 g) all-purpose (plain) flour
1 cup (8 fl oz / 250 ml) milk
½ cup (4 fl oz / 125 ml) white wine
2 teaspoons hot paprika
salt and freshly ground pepper
10 oz (300 g) boned cod
  or other white-fleshed fish
3 oz (90 g) shrimp (prawns) peeled,
  deveined and chopped
½ cup (1 oz / 30 g) chopped parsley
3 oz (90 g) mussels, cooked and finely chopped
flour, for dredging
2 eggs beaten with a little water
breadcrumbs, for coating
oil, for frying

This croquette recipe is based on a flour-and-milk dough.

Vegetable croquettes

Croquetas de verduras

- 1 can (14 oz / 440 g) red kidney beans, drained
- 1 lb (500 g) potatoes, boiled and mashed
- 1 tablespoon finely chopped celery
- 1 tablespoon finely chopped onion
- 1 tablespoon finely chopped green (spring) onion
- 1 tablespoon finely chopped parsley
- 3 eggs
- flour, for dredging
- 3 tablespoons water
- breadcrumbs, for coating
- oil, for frying

Puree kidney beans in a food processor. In a bowl, mix beans thoroughly with potatoes, celery, onions, parsley and 1 egg. Mixture should be firm enough to shape into croquettes; if not, add enough breadcrumbs to form desired consistency.

Shape vegetable mixture into cylindrical croquettes about 3 inches (7.5 cm) long and 1 inch (2.5 cm) in diameter. In a frying pan, heat enough oil to cover croquettes; oil is ready when it reaches 350¡F (180¡C) on a deep-frying thermometer.

In a bowl, lightly beat remaining 2 eggs and water. Dredge croquettes in flour, dip into beaten eggs and then roll in breadcrumbs. Deep-fry until golden brown. Drain on paper towels and serve hot.

Serves 10—12

Batter-fried vegetables

Verduras fritas

In a bowl, whisk cold water with flour and cornstarch until completely smooth. (When you dip a finger into batter, it should run off, leaving just a thin coating on your finger.) Whisk in salt, lemon juice and egg yolk. Refrigerate batter for about 15 minutes.

Pour oil in a frying pan to a depth of 3 inches (7.5 cm) and heat to 350¡F (180¡C) on a deep-frying thermometer. Working in batches, dredge vegetables in seasoned flour, shaking off excess, then dip into batter. Deep-fry vegetables until golden brown. Drain on paper towels. Serve immediately with lemon wedges and garlic mayonnaise.

Serves 15—20

- 1 cup (8 fl oz / 250 ml) cold water
- 1 cup (4 oz / 125 g) all-purpose (plain) flour
- 1/2 cup (2 oz / 60 g) cornstarch (cornflour)
- pinch of salt
- dash of lemon juice
- 1 egg yolk
- 1 eggplant (aubergine), thinly sliced crosswise
- 1/2 cauliflower, cut into small florets, blanched for 3–4 minutes and drained
- 2 large onions, sliced and separated into rings
- 2 zucchini (courgettes), cut into thin strips 2 inches (5 cm) long
- 1 red or green bell pepper (capsicum), cut into strips 2 inches by 3/8 inch (5 cm by 1 cm)
- seasoned flour, for dredging
- oil, for frying
- lemon wedges, for serving
- Garlic mayonnaise, for serving (see page 56)

Hint

This popular dish could be compared with tempura. (Not many people know that tempura did, in fact, originate on the Iberian peninsula, having been introduced to Japan by the Portuguese several hundred years ago.) In Spain, the vegetables are served with lemon wedges or garlic mayonnaise.

Cheese marinated in tarragon and garlic

Cambozola con estragón y ajo

2 cups (16 fl oz / 500 ml) extra-virgin olive oil
1 cup (7 fl oz / 210 ml) tarragon vinegar
2 tablespoons chopped fresh tarragon
or 2 teaspoons dried tarragon
2 teaspoons freshly ground pepper
1 head garlic, each clove smashed but unpeeled
1 lb (500 g) Cambozola cheese,
cut into $^3/_8$-inch (2-cm) cubes
fresh tarragon sprigs, for garnish
roasted red pepper (capsicum) strips
(see page 9), for garnish

Combine olive oil, vinegar, chopped tarragon, pepper and garlic in a jar with a tight-fitting lid and let stand for one week. Strain oil, pour over cheese in a bowl. Cover and marinate for 2 days. Serve garnished with tarragon sprigs and red pepper strips.

Serves 8

Hints

Cambozola is an Italian cheese. Your may prefer to use another tangy, firm-bodied white cheese, or a mixture of two or three types. Try the Spanish queso manchego or use a low-salt feta. You can easily vary this recipe according to taste, but be careful not to use ingredients that will overpower the cheese. Your may also vary the herbs or add two or three fresh or dried chili peppers to the marinade. Sun-dried tomatoes make a great accompaniment.

Mallorcan pizza

Coca mallorquín

To prepare the dough: Whisk the yeast into the milk until frothy, then set aside for 10 minutes. Sift flour and salt into a bowl. Make a well in the center, pour in the oil and add the yeast mixture. Mix in enough cold water to make a soft dough. Knead on a board for 5 minutes or until smooth and elastic. Return to the bowl, cover with a cloth and set aside at room temperature or slightly warmer to rise for 1 hour.

Knead dough again gently, adding olive oil as you work it, and shape with the fingers into a 5-inch (13-cm) round or rectangle that fits a large greased and floured shallow pan about 13 inches by 9 inches (35 cm by 20 cm).

Preheat oven to 400¡F (200¡C / Gas 6). In a bowl, mix bell peppers, onions, tomatoes and parsley with salt to taste. Spread over dough. Bake until crust is golden brown, 30—45 minutes.

Serves 12

FOR DOUGH

1 oz (27 g) fresh yeast or 1/2 oz (12 g) dry yeast
3 tablespoons lukewarm milk
4 cups (1 lb / 500 g) all-purpose (plain) flour
1 1/2 teaspoons salt
3 tablespoons olive oil
cold water

2 tablespoons olive oil
1/2 cup (3 oz / 90 g) diced red bell pepper (capsicum)
1/2 cup (3 oz / 90 g) diced green bell pepper (capsicum)
2 onions, thinly sliced
12 oz (375 g) tomatoes, chopped
2 tablespoons chopped parsley
salt to taste

Meatballs

Albóndigas

1 lb (500 g) ground (minced) pork or beef
½ cup (2 oz / 60 g) finely chopped onion
4 cloves garlic, finely chopped
1 tablespoon chopped parsley
½ cup (2 oz / 60 g) fine breadcrumbs
3 eggs
1 red chili pepper, minced,
or a dash of chili sauce (see page 56)
freshly ground pepper
salt
flour, for coating
oil, for frying

In a bowl, combine all ingredients except flour, mixing thoroughly. Let stand for 30 minutes to allow flavors to blend. In a frying pan, heat enough oil to cover meatballs; oil is ready when it reaches 350¡F (180¡C) on a deep-frying thermometer. Roll meatballs in flour. Deep-fry, turning once, until cooked through. Drain on paper towels and serve immediately.

Serves 12

In Spain one would usually prepare this dish using ground (minced) pork, but beef is a good alternative. The following recipe will produce about 40–50 meatballs if you make them about 1 inch (2.5 cm) in diameter. When served as tapas, meatballs are traditionally presented with garlic mayonnaise (see page 56) as a dip or are reheated in a rich tomato sauce such as simple tomato sauce (see page 56).

Lamb brochettes with rosemary

Pinchos de cordero con romero

Combine all ingredients except lamb in a large glass or ceramic bowl. Add lamb and stir to coat well. Cover and refrigerate overnight. Start a fire in a charcoal grill. Drain lamb, reserving marinade. Thread lamb cubes on skewers. In a small saucepan, bring marinade to a boil. Remove from heat, then set aside. When coals are hot, cook lamb to desired doneness, basting constantly with marinade. Serve at once.

Serves 10

1 cup (2 oz / 60 g) chopped fresh rosemary
2 cloves garlic, finely chopped
juice of 2 lemons
salt and freshly ground pepper
1 cup (8 fl oz / 250 ml) olive oil
2 lb (1 kg) boned lamb or beef loin, cut into 1-inch (2.5-cm) cubes

Hint

To obtain the real flavor of this dish, the meat should be diced and marinated for 24 hours.

Moorish-style kabobs

Pinchos morunos

Since Spain was occupied by the Arabs for eight hundred years, one finds many Moorish influences on Spanish architecture, culture and food. This dish, which has remained popular in Spain throughout the centuries, is almost identical to one found in North Africa, with the notable exception that pork is generally used instead of lamb.

Combine all ingredients except pork in a large glass or ceramic bowl. Add pork and stir to coat well. Cover and refrigerate overnight. Start a fire in a charcoal grill. Drain pork, reserving marinade. Thread pork cubes on skewers. In a small pan, bring marinade to a boil. Remove from heat, then set aside. When coals are hot, cook pork to desired doneness, basting frequently with marinade. Serve at once.

Serves 8

1/2 cup (4 fl oz / 125 ml) olive oil
1 teaspoon chopped fresh thyme
1 teaspoon chili powder
1 teaspoon paprika
2 teaspoons ground cumin
1 teaspoon freshly ground pepper
1 teaspoon salt
1 1/2 teaspoons chopped parsley
1–1 1/2 lb (500–750 g) lean pork, cut into 3/4-inch (2-cm) cubes

Chicken legs

Piernas de pollo

16 chicken legs, skin removed
flour, for dredging
olive oil, for frying
1 onion, finely chopped
1 tablespoon chopped garlic
1 lb (500 g) canned whole peeled plum (Roma) tomatoes
1 cup (8 fl oz / 250 ml) chicken stock
salt and freshly ground pepper

Preheat oven to 300¡F (150¡C / Gas 2). Dredge chicken legs in flour. In a frying pan over medium heat, warm oil. Fry chicken, turning as needed, until evenly browned. Remove from pan. Pour off excess oil. Return pan to medium heat and saut onion and garlic until onion is transparent. Add tomatoes and cook for 15 minutes. Remove from heat and puree in a blender or food processor with chicken stock. Season with salt and pepper.

Arrange chicken legs in a baking dish and cover with tomato sauce. Cover with aluminum foil and bake for 1 hour. Remove foil, turn chicken in sauce, pour off any excess liquid and bake until chicken is tender, about 30 minutes. Serve immediately.

Serves 8

Chicken salad

Ensalada de pollo

Remove meat from the chicken, discarding skin and bones. Cut into 1-inch (2.5-cm) dices. Place in a bowl and combine with remaining ingredients. Cover and allow to stand in refrigerator for 30 minutes before serving.

Serves 12

2–3 lb (1–1.5 kg) whole chicken, roasted
4 celery stalks, finely diced
1 apple, peeled and diced
2 red bell peppers (capsicums), seeded and finely diced
1 cucumber, peeled, seeded and finely diced
1 pear, peeled, cored and diced
10 green (spring) onions, green tops only, finely chopped
1 cup (8 fl oz / 250 ml) Garlic mayonnaise (see page 56)
salt and freshly ground pepper

Deep-fried squid

Calamares a la romana

2 lb (1 kg) fresh squid (calamari), cleaned (see page 58)
flour, for dredging
4 eggs mixed with 2 tablespoons water
breadcrumbs, for coating
oil, for frying

The secret to making this dish is the heat of the oil and the speed at which the squid is cooked. It should be deep-fried at 350—400¡F (180—200¡C) for no more than 1 minute; this ensures that the squid will be tender. If cooked for any longer, the squid tends to become rubbery. Note also that the smaller the squid, the more tender they are likely to be.

Pour oil into a frying pan to a depth of 3 inches (7.5 cm). Heat oil to correct temperature when measured on a deep-frying thermometer. Slice squid bodies into rings about $^{1}{}_{4}$ inch (6 mm) thick. Dredge rings in flour, dip into egg mixture and then coat with breadcrumbs. Fry squid for 1 minute. Drain on paper towels and serve immediately.

Serves 8

Chili shrimp with cream sauce

Gambas picantes con nata

In a wok over high heat, warm 1 tablespoon of oil. When oil is smoking, add half of shrimp, half of ginger and half of garlic. Stir for 1 minute, then cover and cook until shrimp are just cooked through, 3—4 minutes; don t overcook. Transfer to a bowl and repeat with remaining shrimp, ginger and garlic; remove from wok.

Add chili sauce and cream to wok, bring to a boil and cook for 4—5 minutes to reduce. Tip into a bowl and serve as a dipping sauce for shrimp.

Serves 8

- 2 tablespoons olive oil
- 24 large shrimp (prawns), shells intact
- 1 tablespoon peeled and finely chopped fresh ginger
- 1 tablespoon finely chopped garlic
- 1 tablespoon chili sauce (see page 56)
- 1¼ cups (10 fl oz / 300 ml) heavy (double) cream

Hint

It's best to prepare this dish in a large wok with a lid. The flavors of the chili sauce, garlic and ginger permeate the shrimp, and the juice given off by the shrimp enhances the sauce.

Grilled shrimp

Gambas a la plancha

8 cloves garlic, coarsely chopped
½ cup (4 fl oz / 125 ml) olive oil
2 lb (1 kg) shrimp (prawns), shells intact
chopped parsley, for garnish
Garlic mayonnaise (see page 56), for serving

In a small bowl, marinate garlic in olive oil for at least 30 minutes. Oil a heavy large frying pan and place over medium-high heat. Add as many shrimp as will fit in one layer. Drizzle about 1 teaspoon of olive oil over each shrimp, add some garlic and cook for 2 minutes. Turn shrimp, drizzle with a little more olive oil and cook for 2 more minutes, then remove from heat. Do not overcook or shrimp will become mushy.

Wipe pan with a paper towel and repeat process until all shrimp are cooked. Keep shrimp warm in a low oven while you cook remainder. Sprinkle with chopped parsley and serve with garlic mayonnaise.

Serves 8

Hints

A la plancha simply means that a food is grilled, a very common method of cooking seafood and steaks in Spain. The best way to achieve the same results is to use a very heavy, large frying pan that has been lightly oiled, with small amounts of oil added during cooking. The shrimp are cooked a few at a time, so each remains in contact with the bottom of the pan. Alternatively, the shrimp can be cooked on a barbecue and basted with olive oil and garlic. In Spain, shrimp are usually eaten from the shell.

Garlic shrimp

Gambas al Ajillo

Divide garlic and chilies among 8 individual, flameproof ramekins. To each ramekin add enough oil to just cover shrimp when added later. Heat over high heat until garlic turns golden brown. Add shrimp and remove from heat after 1 minute. Sprinkle with coarse salt and serve immediately.

Serves 8

8 cloves garlic, finely chopped
4 red chili peppers, seeded and chopped
olive oil as needed
2 lb (1 kg) shrimp (prawns), peeled and deveined
coarse salt

Hint

Serve with plenty of crusty bread.

Sangría

Red wine punch

This is a very sweet red wine punch that's perfect for a warm afternoon as it is cooling and refreshing. Be ware though, it's more alcoholic than its mild taste suggests!

Mix wine, brandy and sugar, stirring to dissolve sugar. Chill well. Just before serving, add the soda water and fruit.

Makes 6 cups

4 cups (32 fl oz / 1 L) light-bodied red wine, well chilled
3/4 cup (6 fl oz / 180 ml) Spanish or other brandy
1/2 cup (4 oz / 120 g) superfine (caster) sugar
2 cups (16 fl oz / 500 ml) soda water
1 orange, sliced
6–8 strawberries, halved

Batter-fried fish

Pescado frito

- 1 cup (8 fl oz / 250 ml) cold water
- 1 cup (4 oz / 125 g) all-purpose (plain) flour
- ½ cup (2 oz / 60 g) cornstarch (cornflour)
- pinch of salt
- dash of lemon juice
- 1 egg yolk
- 1 lb (500 g) bream, porgy or other lean fish
- oil, for frying
- flour, for dredging

In a bowl, whisk cold water with flour and cornstarch until completely smooth. When you dip a finger into batter, it should run off, leaving just a thin coating on your finger. Whisk in salt, lemon juice and egg yolk. Cover and refrigerate batter for about 15 minutes.

Cut fish into strips about $2^{1}{}_{4}$ by $1^{1}{}_{4}$ inches (6 cm by 3 cm). Pour 3 inches (7.5 cm) oil in a frying pan and heat to 400¡F (200¡C) on a deep-frying thermometer. Dredge fish in flour and then coat with batter. Fry until golden brown on both sides. Drain on paper towels and serve immediately.

Serves 8

Fish puffs

Buñuelos de pescado

- 1 lb (500 g) potatoes, peeled, boiled and mashed
- 8 oz (250 g) cod, steamed and boned
- 1 clove garlic, finely chopped
- 1 tablespoon chopped parsley
- pinch of salt
- pinch of pepper
- 4 egg yolks
- oil, for frying

Many variations of buñuelos, savory or sweet, are prepared in Spain. With a little imagination, many alternatives of this simple dish can be created.

Place potatoes in a bowl. Crumble cod into potatoes and then add garlic, parsley, salt and pepper. Stir in egg yolks, mixing thoroughly until smooth. In a frying pan, heat about $1^{1}{}_{4}$ inches (3 cm) oil until hot. Oil is ready when a bread cube dropped in hot oil sizzles on contact. Drop about $1^{1}{}_{2}$ teaspoons of fish mixture at a time into hot oil and fry until golden on all sides. Drain on paper towels. Serve hot.

Serves 8

Mussels in tomato sauce

Mejillones Madrileños

Steam mussels in a wide saucepan with about 2 inches (5 cm) water, removing them as they open and discarding any that do not open. Refresh under cold running water and set aside. Discard shell halves to which mussels are not attached.

Heat olive oil in a large frying pan over medium heat and saut onion and garlic until transparent. Add remaining ingredients except cheese and cook until reduced to a smooth sauce.

Arrange mussels on a baking sheet. Cover each with tomato sauce and top with a sprinkling of cheese. Brown under broiler (grill). Serve at once.

Serves 8

- 40 mussels, scrubbed and debearded
- 3 tablespoons olive oil
- 1 onion, finely chopped
- 4 cloves garlic, finely chopped
- 1 lb (500 g) canned whole peeled plum (Roma) tomatoes
- 1/2 cup (3/4 oz / 20 g) chopped parsley
- 2 bay leaves
- salt and freshly ground pepper
- freshly grated Parmesan cheese, for sprinkling

Mussels marinated in vinaigrette sauce

Mejillones en escabeche

40 mussels, scrubbed and debearded

FOR ESCABECHE

1½ cups (12 fl oz / 375 ml) olive oil

¾ cup (6 fl oz / 180 ml) red wine vinegar

½ cup (2 oz / 60 g) minced onion

2 tablespoons chopped parsley

2 teaspoons hot paprika or chili powder

juice of 1 lemon

salt and freshly ground pepper

Steam mussels in a wide saucepan with about 2 inches (5 cm) water, removing them as they open and discarding any that do not open. Refresh under cold running water and discard shell halves to which mussels are not attached.

To make escabeche: Combine all ingredients in a glass or ceramic bowl. Add mussels, cover and refrigerate for at least 12 hours or, preferably, 24 hours. Serve mussels cold in their marinade.

Serves 8

Stuffed lobster tails

Langosta rellena

Remove meat from each lobster tail, leaving shell intact. Blanch shells in a saucepan of boiling water for 2—3 minutes. Drain and rinse thoroughly. Remove tough outer skin from lobster meat and cut meat crosswise into slices 1 2—3 4 inch (1—2 cm) thick.

In a saucepan over medium heat, warm oil. Saut onions, garlic, ginger, cilantro roots and white part of green onions for 4 minutes. Add cognac and cook for 1 minute. Add paprika, chili sauce, bell pepper puree, tomato puree and vinegar and simmer for 15—20 minutes.

In another frying pan, melt butter and gently saut lobster slices with green onion tops and coriander leaves. When lobster has changed color and is half cooked, drain and add lobster to sauce. Simmer until lobster is opaque throughout (do not overcook). Remove lobster from sauce and arrange in shells. Top with sauce and serve.

Serves 8

8 small lobster tails, about 3 oz (100 g) each
1/4 cup (2 fl oz / 60 ml) olive oil
2 onions, finely chopped
4 cloves garlic, finely chopped
1 tablespoon peeled and finely chopped fresh ginger
2 tablespoons chopped fresh cilantro (coriander), plus 2 tablespoons roots, chopped
4 scallions (shallots / spring onions), finely chopped, plus green tops, finely chopped
1/2 cup (4 fl oz / 125 ml) cognac
1 tablespoon hot paprika
2 tablespoons chili sauce (see page 56)
4 red bell peppers (capsicums), roasted, peeled and seeded (see page 9), then pureed
1 cup (8 oz / 250 g) whole peeled tomatoes, pureed
2 tablespoons red wine vinegar
2 tablespoons butter

Mixed seafood vinaigrette

Salpicón

- 1 cup (8 fl oz / 250 ml) olive oil
- juice of 1 lemon
- $^1/_3$ cup (3 fl oz / 90 ml) white wine vinegar
- $^1/_2$ cup (2 oz / 60 g) finely chopped onion
- 2 red bell peppers (capsicums), roasted, peeled and seeded (see page 9), then cut into thin strips
- 1 lb (500 g) cooked lobster
- 1 lb (500 g) cooked shrimp (prawns), shelled and deveined, leaving tails intact
- 7 oz (220 g) cooked crabmeat
- 7 oz (220 g) cooked mussels (discard shell halves to which mussels are not attached)
- 7 oz (220 g) squid bodies, cut into rings, poached in white wine for 1 minute and drained
- 7 oz (220 g) cooked firm, white-fleshed fish

In a large glass or ceramic bowl, combine olive oil, lemon juice, vinegar, onion and bell peppers and mix well. Fold in seafood. Cover and refrigerate for several hours or as long as overnight, turning occasionally. Serve chilled.

Serves 10

Seafood medley

Zarzuela tapa

Clean crabs and cut down center so that each half has a claw attached. Set aside. Heat oil in a large frying pan over medium heat. Saut onion and garlic for 2 minutes. Add shrimp, crabs (if raw) and fish cubes. Add about half of fish stock and simmer, removing seafood as it is almost cooked. When all seafood is cooked, add remaining fish stock to pan along with tomatoes, chilies, cognac, wine and parsley and simmer for 10 minutes. Add mussels and cook, removing them as they open and discarding any that do not open.

Divide mussels among 8 bowls. Add crab (if cooked), shrimp and fish to simmering sauce and cook for 2 minutes. Divide seafood and sauce among bowls and serve at once.

Serves 10

4 small crabs about 4 oz (125 g) in total or 1 lb (500 g) crabmeat, raw or cooked
2 tablespoons olive oil
1 onion, finely diced
4 cloves garlic, finely chopped
8 jumbo shrimp (king prawns), heads removed, leaving shells intact
8 oz (250 g) tuna or other firm-fleshed fish such as cod, cut into $^3/_4$-inch (2-cm) cubes
1 cup (8 fl oz / 250 ml) fish stock
1 lb (500 g) canned whole peeled plum (Roma) tomatoes
3 red chili peppers, seeded and chopped, or 1 tablespoon chili sauce (see page 56)
$^1/_4$ cup (2 fl oz / 60 ml) cognac
$^1/_2$ cup (4 fl oz / 125 ml) dry white wine
1 tablespoon chopped parsley
32 mussels, scrubbed and debearded
salt

Clams in white wine sauce

Almejas a la marinera

- olive oil as needed
- 1 onion, finely chopped
- 6 cloves garlic, finely chopped
- 1 tablespoon flour
- 1½ cups (12 fl oz / 375 ml) medium-dry white wine
- ½ cup (1 oz / 30 g) minced parsley, plus extra, for garnish
- 1 chili pepper, seeded
- salt and freshly ground pepper
- 36 small clams, cleaned and soaked

To clean and soak clams: Scrub clam shells and place in a container of lightly salted water and let stand overnight in a cool place. Heat a little oil in a frying pan over medium heat. Add onion and garlic and cook until transparent. Stir in flour and cook for 1 minute. Add remaining ingredients except clams and cook for 10 minutes. Add clams and cook, removing them as they open and discarding any that do not open. Sprinkle with a little more parsley and serve.

Serves 4

Barbecued baby octopus

Pulpo a la plancha

- 1 cup (8 fl oz / 250 ml) olive oil
- 4 cloves garlic, finely chopped
- 4½ lb (2 kg) tenderized baby octopus (see page 58 for instructions)
- ¼ cup (2 fl oz / 60 ml) lemon juice
- Sweet chili sauce (see page 56)

For octopus Galacian style (*pulpo a la Gallega*), add 1 tablespoon hot paprika to olive oil and garlic mixture.

In a bowl, combine olive oil and garlic and set aside for 3—4 hours. Remove and discard octopus heads. Remove the little hard ball, or beak, in the center of each octopus. Prepare a fire in a grill and heat grill plate until very hot. Evenly cover it with half the oil and garlic mixture. Place all octopus on grill plate and sprinkle with lemon juice (a lot of liquid will exude from the octopus and the hot plate will cool down considerably). Cook until the octopus is barely cooked through, about 2 minutes on each side.

Remove octopus and scrape down the plate; allow it to heat up again. When very hot, cover it with remaining oil and garlic mixture. When oil begins to smoke, grill octopus underside down until the ends of the tentacles are crunchy. Serve immediately with sweet chili sauce.

Serves 8

Clams in piquant tomato sauce

Almejas al diablo

Heat a little oil in a frying pan over medium heat. Fry onion and garlic until transparent. Add tomatoes, chili, bay leaves, parsley, wine and salt and pepper to taste. Bring to boil over a high heat and allow to reduce slightly.

Add the clams, cover pan tightly and simmer until clams have opened. Remove clams as they open and discard any that do not open.

Divide clams among individual bowls and top with sauce. Serve immediately.

Serves 4

olive oil as needed
1 onion, finely chopped
2 cloves garlic, finely chopped
8 oz (250 g) canned plum (Roma) tomatoes, minced
1 or 2 red chili peppers, seeded
2 bay leaves
1/4 cup (1/2 oz / 15 g) finely chopped parsley
1 cup (8 fl oz / 250 ml) dry white wine
salt and white pepper
36 small clams, soaked (see below)

Hint

There is a great variety of shellfish in Spain; almejas are a type of clam, usually quite small. This clam recipe is used in Spain for this variety, so it is best to select the smallest type available at your market. This dish will be equally good with larger clams. Just remember to reduce the number of clams you use according to their size.

Soaking Clams

Sand released from clams during cooking can ruin a dish. Soaking the clams in advance allows them to expel the sand. First scrub the shells, then place clams in a container of lightly salted water and let stand overnight in a cool place.

Mussels steamed in spicy tomato sauce

Mejillones en salsa picante de tomate

- 2 tablespoons olive oil
- 2 onions, finely chopped
- 6 cloves garlic, finely chopped
- 1 tablespoon peeled and finely chopped fresh ginger
- 1 bunch cilantro (coriander), roots and leaves finely chopped and kept separate
- 1 lb (500 g) canned whole peeled tomatoes, pureed
- 1 tablespoon chili sauce (see page 56)
- 1¼ cups (10 fl oz / 300 ml) dry white wine
- salt
- 2 lb (1 kg) mussels, scrubbed and debearded
- cilantro (coriander) sprigs, for garnish

In a pot that is large enough to accommodate all ingredients, warm oil over medium heat. Saut onions, garlic, ginger and cilantro roots in olive oil for 3—4 minutes. Add tomatoes, chili sauce, wine and salt to taste and simmer for about 10 minutes.

Add cilantro leaves and mussels. Increase heat and cover pot tightly. Have 8 small bowls ready. As mussels open, remove them from pot and divide among bowls, checking pot every 2 minutes (if opened mussels are allowed to remain in liquid, they will shrink and toughen). It will take 6—10 minutes for all mussels to open; discard any that do not open after this time.

Pour sauce over mussels. Garnish with cilantro sprigs and serve with warm, crusty bread to soak up the sauce.

Serves 8

Oyster platter

Plato variado de ostras

Arrange 18 oysters on a platter large enough to accommodate them. Place ^{1}2 teaspoon of red caviar on 6 oysters, covering half of each, and ^{1}2 teaspoon of black caviar on other half. Top up shells of next 6 oysters with tomato cocktail mixture. Squeeze lime juice over last 6 oysters and sprinkle with a little pepper.

Place remaining 18 oysters on a broiler (grill) pan. In a saucepan, combine half of b chamel sauce with half of cheddar cheese. Heat gently, stirring occasionally, until cheese is melted and combined with sauce. Spoon cheese mixture over 6 oysters and top with Parmesan cheese.

In a saucepan, blanch spinach in boiling water for 2 minutes. Drain and squeeze dry. In a saucepan combine spinach with remaining b chamel and cheddar cheese. Heat gently, stirring occasionally, until cheese has melted. Spoon spinach mixture over next 6 oysters. Top remaining 6 oysters with bacon and a few drops of Worcestershire sauce.

Place pan under broiler (grill) and cook oysters until sauces begin to brown and bubble. Arrange on platter with other oysters. Garnish with lemon wedges and serve.

Serves 6

rock salt
36 oysters in the half shell
3 teaspoons red caviar
3 teaspoons black caviar
1 cup tomato cocktail mixture (below)
1 lime, halved
freshly ground pepper
1/2 cup (4 fl oz / 125 ml) prepared béchamel sauce
1/2 cup (4 oz / 125 g) grated sharp cheddar cheese
3 teaspoons grated Parmesan cheese
1 cup (2 oz / 60 g) finely chopped spinach leaves
1 tablespoon diced bacon
3 teaspoons Worcestershire sauce
lemon wedges, for garnish

FOR TOMATO COCKTAIL MIXTURE
dash Worcestershire sauce
2 drops tabasco sauce
1/4 fl oz (8 ml) lemon juice
salt and pepper, to taste
1 cup (8 fl oz / 250 ml) tomato juice

Tomato cocktail

To make tomato cocktail mixture: In a small bowl, mix a dash of worcestershire sauce, tabasco sauce, lemon juice, and salt and pepper to taste. Mix until well combined and top with tomato juice.

Squid and octopus salad

Ensalada de calamares y pulpo

3 lb (1.5 kg) baby octopus, tenderized (see page 58)
3 lb (1.5 kg) squid
1 cup (8 fl oz / 250 ml) white wine vinegar
1 onion studded with 12 cloves
6 bay leaves
12 white peppercorns
1 teaspoon salt
1 tablespoon finely chopped fresh dill
1 cup (8 fl oz / 250 ml) olive oil
½ cup (4 fl oz / 125 ml) freshly squeezed lemon juice
lemon wedges, for serving
freshly ground pepper

Clean octopus, removing and discarding heads. Clean squid thoroughly, discarding heads but retaining tentacles. In a large pot, bring 3—4 quarts (3—4 L) of water to boil. Add vinegar, clove-studded onion, bay leaves, peppercorns and salt boil for about 10 minutes. Add squid and octopus and cook until tender, about 20—30 minutes. Lift squid and octopus from liquid and refresh under cold running water. Remove any skin from seafood. Discard contents of pot. Cut octopus and squid tentacles into chunks and slice squid bodies into very thin rings.

In a glass or ceramic bowl, mix seafood with dill, olive oil and lemon juice. Cover and marinate overnight in refrigerator. Serve with lemon wedges and pepper.

Serves 8—10

Variation

Substitute lime juice for the lemon juice and fresh cilantro (coriander) for dill; add 1 tablespoon chili sauce (see page 56) to the marinade.

Spicy marinated sardines

Sardinas en escabeche picante

Clean sardines and cut off and discard heads. Rinse and dry fish. Pour enough oil in a frying pan to cover bottom generously and place pan over medium heat. Dredge fish in seasoned flour, shaking off excess. Brown quickly on both sides; do not cook through. Drain on paper towels.

To make escabeche: Heat oil in a nonaluminum pot until moderately hot. Add garlic, onions, ginger and cilantro root and cook for 5 minutes. Stir in tomato puree, tomato paste, vinegar, bay leaves, chili sauce, cilantro and salt to taste, and simmer for 30 minutes.

Meanwhile, layer sardines compactly in an earthenware or stainless steel bowl, interspersing layers with red bell pepper strips. Pour marinade over sardines, making sure all are well covered. Let cool, then cover and refrigerate for at least 4 days before serving; during this time, the sardine bones soften completely. Serve chilled.

Serves 15—20

2 lb (1 kg) fresh sardines
olive oil, for frying
flour, seasoned with salt and a little chili powder, for dredging

FOR ESCABECHE
4 cups (32 fl oz / 1 L) olive oil
20 cloves garlic, peels intact, crushed
2 large onions, thinly sliced
1 tablespoon peeled and minced fresh ginger
1 tablespoon chopped cilantro (coriander) root
1 cup (8 fl oz / 250 ml) tomato puree
2 tablespoons tomato paste
3 cups (24 fl oz / 750 ml) red wine vinegar
12 bay leaves
1–2 tablespoons chili sauce (see page 56)
2 tablespoons chopped cilantro (coriander)
salt
4 red bell peppers (capsicums) roasted, peeled and seeded (see page 9), then cut into strips

This is an adaptation of the traditional Spanish method of preserving sardines. If you prefer the Spanish marinade, omit the ginger, chili sauce and cilantro, and add sprigs of fresh thyme and oregano with the vinegar.

sauces

The following chili sauces are Asian style, but make a delicious addition to tapas recipes. The simple tomato sauce (salsa de tomate), the zesty tomato sauce (salsa picante) and mayonnaise (salsa mayonesa) are traditional accompaniments and ingredients found in many Spanish recipes. They make ideal dipping sauces for tapas.

Chili sauce

1 lb (500 g) red chili peppers
2½ cups (20 fl oz / 625 ml) water
1 tablespoon white vinegar
1 teaspoon superfine (caster) sugar
2 tablespoons peanut oil
½ cup (4 fl oz / 125 ml) boiling water

Remove stems from chili peppers. Remove seeds if you want a less fiery sauce. Place chilies and water in a saucepan over medium heat and bring to a boil. Cover, reduce heat to simmer and cook until chilies are soft, about 15 minutes. Drain. Working in batches, place chilies in a food processor and process until smooth. Add vinegar, sugar, peanut oil and boiling water and process to combine. Pour into sterilized jars, seal and refrigerate for up to 1 month.

Makes about 1½ cups (12 fl oz / 375 ml)

Zesty tomato sauce

This sauce is a delicious accompaniment to stuffed artichokes (see page 10).

olive oil
1 onion, finely chopped
3 cloves garlic, finely chopped
1 lb (500 g) canned tomatoes, pureed
1 red chili pepper, seeded and chopped
2 bay leaves
salt and freshly ground black pepper

Heat a little olive oil in a frying pan over medium heat. Fry onion and garlic until transparent. Add tomatoes, chili, bay leaves and salt and pepper to taste and cook until reduced to a good sauce consistency, 20—30 minutes.

Makes 3 cups (24 fl oz / 750 ml)

Sweet chili sauce

1 tablespoon chili sauce (see chili sauce recipe)
1 tablespoon brown sugar
2 tablespoons granulated sugar
3 cups (24 fl oz / 750 ml) white wine vinegar

Combine all ingredients in a non aluminum saucepan and boil for about 10 minutes. Let cool. The sauce keeps in the refrigerator for up to 3 months.

Makes 3 cups (24 fl oz / 750 ml)

Simple tomato sauce

This rich sauce is the perfect accompaniment to the meatballs recipe (see page 36).

2 cloves garlic, finely chopped or pressed
1 onion, finely chopped
olive oil as needed
1 lb (500 g) canned tomatoes, pureed
2 or 3 bay leaves
salt and freshly ground pepper
aromatic herb such as thyme (optional)

Warm a little olive oil in a frying pan over medium heat. Fry onion and garlic until transparent. Add tomatoes, bay leaves, salt and pepper to taste and herb (if using). Simmer for 30 minutes on low to medium heat.

Makes 3 cups (24 fl oz / 750 ml)

Variation: For an alternative sauce, in a saucepan, combine 6 finely chopped garlic cloves, 1 tablespoon chopped parsley and ½ cup (4 oz / 125 g) melted butter. Simmer for 2 minutes to allow the flavors to blend. Serve hot.

Mayonnaise and garlic mayonnaise

Both mayonnaise and garlic mayonnaise are common ingredients in, and accompaniments to, tapas. While both are available in prepared form, you will achieve infinitely better results by preparing your own. Both regular and garlic mayonnaise keep in the refrigerator for at least a week, tightly covered.

3 egg yolks
1 tablespoon white wine vinegar
pinch of sugar
salt and freshly ground pepper
2 cups (16 fl oz / 500 ml) olive oil
1 teaspoon lemon juice

Combine egg yolks, vinegar, mustard, sugar and salt and pepper to taste in a large bowl and whisk to blend. Whisk in oil, a few drops at a time, gradually increasing to a very slow stream as mixture emulsifies. Mix in lemon juice. Taste and adjust seasonings if necessary.

To make in a food processor, add egg yolks to bowl and process while pouring in oil a little at a time. When mixture begins to emulsify and thicken, alternately add remaining ingredients with olive oil until oil is incorporated. Taste and adjust seasonings if necessary.

If mixture separates (which usually occurs when oil is added too quickly), immediately stop mixing, transfer mixture into a bowl, add 2 more egg yolks and mix in remaining ingredients. Then, very slowly and carefully add separated mixture to new mixture.

For garlic mayonnaise, add 2 or more minced garlic cloves to egg yolk mixture.

Makes 3 cups (24 fl oz / 750 ml)

glossary

Chili peppers Red chilies are frequently used in tapas. They are more often used in their dried form to add tang to a dish rather than to make it spicy-hot. Having given this advice, as you will note, I completely ignore it and tend to be heavy-handed with chili in a number of recipes. This is a personal preference and one that has always seemed to meet the approval of people who sample the dishes. Rather than use dried or fresh chilies, however, I often add their flavor in the form of chili sauce, containing red chilies, salt and vinegar. I find that the best way to keep chili on hand is simply to have a jar of chili sauce in the refrigerator. It keeps almost indefinitely, has a great flavor and is available from Asian markets and many delicatessens.

Chorizo This Spanish pork sausage often has an orange tint due to the presence of paprika. It has many uses and is often sliced and eaten cold or fried and served with bread. Chorizo and other Spanish sausages are available at Spanish, Portuguese or South American delicatessens.

Clams Most tapas recipes use small clams. If you are unable to find them, use a larger variety and reduce the quantities of other ingredients in the recipes. But a word of warning: the larger clams are tougher.

Cognac This is specified in a number of recipes. If you can find good Spanish brandy, it is the preferred ingredient. You can also use French cognac or brandy. Avoid using cheap brandy, as it can mar the flavor of a dish.

Octopus If you cannot obtain tenderized baby octopus or if you have a ready supply of larger fresh octopus, follow this procedure. Holding octopus firmly, beat or throw it forcefully against a hard surface (such as concrete) about 30 or 40 times. Clean each octopus throughouly and discard the head. Remove the little hard ball (or beak) in the center of octopus and cut off the last ¾ inch (2 cm) of tentacles. Half fill a pot large enough to accommodate octopus with water and bring it to a boil. Immerse octopus in boiling water for 30 seconds, then remove it. Bring water back to the boil and repeat the process 3 more times. Bring water to the boil again and add for each 2 L water, a peeled onion studded with 6 cloves, 1 bay leaf, 6 white peppercorns and 2 tablespoons vinegar. Add octopus and simmer gently. There is no exact formula as to how long to cook octopus; it will depend on how successful you have been in tenderizing it and on the thickness of the tentacles. After one hour, remove a piece of octopus and bite into it to test for tenderness; repeat this process every 15 minutes or so until octopus is tender. (Cooking can take one hour or as long as three.) Drain cooked octopus and cut tentacles into bite-size cross-sections.

Olive oil Where olive oil is specified, it is important to use Spanish olive oil. It has a distinct flavor essential to many of these recipes.

Squid Pay a little extra and buy small, fresh squid rather than frozen. You have to clean them yourself, but the reward is an infinitely better flavor. To clean squid, pull head and attached intestines from tubelike body. Remove and discard long, thin cartilage. Cut off wings from body if desired and remove eyes and beak from mouth. With your fingers, pull skin from body. Use body tube and tentacles as directed in recipes after rinsing under cold running water.

Serrano Serrano and jam n serrano are high-quality hams from the mountain regions of Spain. Proscuitto, an Italian ham, is an adequate substitute.

Tocino This type of cured pork is similar to bacon, with a subtly different flavor. It is often sold in Mediterranean delicatessens, but if it is not available, use bacon or pancetta.

Tomatoes When tasty vine-ripened tomatoes are unavailable, use a good-quality canned variety for a superior flavor.

index

Guide to weights and measures

The conversions given in the recipes in this book are approximate. Whichever system you use, remember to follow it consistently, thereby ensuring that the proportions are consistent throughout a recipe.

WEIGHTS

Imperial	Metric
1/3 oz	10 g
1/2 oz	15 g
3/4 oz	20 g
1 oz	30 g
2 oz	60 g
3 oz	90 g
4 oz (1/4 lb)	125 g
5 oz (1/3 lb)	150 g
6 oz	180 g
7 oz	220 g
8 oz (1/2 lb)	250 g
9 oz	280 g
10 oz	300 g
11 oz	330 g
12 oz (3/4 lb)	375 g
16 oz (1 lb)	500 g
2 lb	1 kg
3 lb	1.5 kg
4 lb	2 kg

VOLUME

Imperial	Metric	Cup
1 fl oz	30 ml	
2 fl oz	60 ml	1/4
3 fl oz	90 ml	1/3
4 fl oz	125 ml	1/2
5 fl oz	150 ml	2/3
6 fl oz	180 ml	3/4
8 fl oz	250 ml	1
10 fl oz	300 ml	1 1/4
12 fl oz	375 ml	1 1/2
13 fl oz	400 ml	1 2/3
14 fl oz	440 ml	1 3/4
16 fl oz	500 ml	2
24 fl oz	750 ml	3
32 fl oz	1L	4

USEFUL CONVERSIONS

1/4 teaspoon	1.25 ml
1/2 teaspoon	2.5 ml
1 teaspoon	5 ml
1 Australian tablespoon	20 ml (4 teaspoons)
1 UK/US tablespoon	15 ml (3 teaspoons)

Butter/Shortening

1 tablespoon	1/2 oz	15 g
1 1/2 tablespoons	3/4 oz	20 g
2 tablespoons	1 oz	30 g
3 tablespoons	1 1/2 oz	45 g

OVEN TEMPERATURE GUIDE

The Celsius (¡C) and Fahrenheit (¡F) temperatures in this chart apply to most electric ovens. Decrease by 25¡F or 10¡C for a gas oven or refer to the manufacturer s temperature guide. For temperatures below 325¡F (160¡C), do not decrease the given temperature.

Oven description	°C	°F	Gas Mark
Cool	110	225	1/4
	130	250	1/2
Very slow	140	275	1
	150	300	2
Slow	170	325	3
Moderate	180	350	4
	190	375	5
Moderately Hot	200	400	6
Fairly Hot	220	425	7
Hot	230	450	8
Very Hot	240	475	9
Extremely Hot	250	500	10

First published in the United States in 2002 by Periplus Editions (HK) Ltd., with editorial offices at 153 Milk Street, Boston, Massachusetts 02109 and 130 Joo Seng Road #06-01/03 Olivine Building Singapore 368357

Commissioned by Deborah Nixon; Text: Vicki Liley; Photographer: Ben Dearnley; Stylist: Vicki Liley; Design Concepts: Kerry Klinner; Editor: Carolyn Miller; Production Manager: Sally Stokes; Project Co-ordinator: Alexandra Nahlous

Printed in India